Bamburgh, Seahouses the Farne Islands

GUIDE AND SHORT HISTORY

Catherine Bowen & Steve Newman   Photography by Brian Young

Longstone lighthouse with Atlantic grey seals (Simon Fraser)

Bamburgh

Bamburgh owes its existence to the castle, which as early as AD 547 was the site of the royal palace of the Saxon King Ida, who ruled for twelve years. It appears that at this time, Bamburgh was called Dynguoaroy and its present name originates from Queen Bebba, the wife of Ida's grandson Ethelfrith, who named it Bebbanburgh in her honour. Over time, it became known as Bamburgh.

In the early middle ages, it was one of the most prosperous towns in England, honoured with a market and a Member of Parliament. In 1121, Henry I granted the lands to the Augustinians, who held them until the dissolution of the monasteries by Henry VIII. In 1265, a Dominican friary was built in what is now the western edge of the village and a leper hospital set up, which closed in the fourteenth century.

The lands were then owned by the Forster family, who lived in Bamburgh Hall just to the right of the church, until the eighteenth century when they came under the ownership of Lord Crewe, the Bishop of Durham, who married Dorothy Forster. Her niece, also called Dorothy, is renowned locally as a Northumberland heroine who rescued her brother, Tom, from Newgate jail in London after the failed 1715 Jacobite rebellion. Disguised as a servant, she rode to London with the village blacksmith from nearby Adderstone and rescued her brother in a daring operation involving duplicate keys with her maid's assistance.

Lord Crewe established a trust to improve the village and there is a hotel named after him by The Grove. In 1894, the trust sold the castle to Lord Armstrong, the wealthy Victorian industrialist, who restored the castle to its present state while living at Cragside, near Rothbury. His son continued this work and the castle and estate are still run by the Armstrong Family.

Car parking and toilets

Thousands of people can descend on Bamburgh during the summer, so car parking space is at a premium. In the village, parking spaces are limited. Please park with consideration for the villagers by not blocking gateways or entrances - remembering that the traffic wardens from Berwick-upon-Tweed are often in the village!

There are two small car parks down The Wynding that give direct access to the beach. The main car park for the village is opposite the castle. This pay and display car park is probably the best option as you can walk into the village from here. Before you leave this car park look over the back wall and you will see a medieval dovecote. The castle has its own car parking up the hill. There is a large 'Honesty Box' car park just past the castle on the road to Seahouses. A short walk across the dunes takes you to the beach. There are public toilets here as well as toilets in the village just down from the church opposite The Grove.

From left: Detail from the village pant in The Grove, Bamburgh / Bamburgh Castle from the village / Medieval Dovecote / Front Street, Bamburgh

The Parish Church of St. Aidan

St. Aidan's Parish Church is often referred to as one of the most beautiful churches in the country. It stands in an ideal setting surrounded by the countryside travelled by St. Aidan and St. Oswald on missionary journeys, with the Holy Island of Lindisfarne, 'the cradle of English Christianity', visible to the north. The imposing, but welcoming, inner porch was added in 1963 and it is important that you close the door when you enter the church so that the swallows can't fly in. Inside it is surprisingly spacious, with a simplicity and beauty that should be experienced first hand. On walking up the path, it is noticeable that the chancel at the eastern end is almost as big as the rest of the church. This shows the wealth and power of the Augustinian friars who built this extension in the thirteenth century, probably for their own use.

St. Aidan built the original Saxon mission church, probably a wooden building, in AD 635 when he came here from the monastery on Iona. When St. Aidan was ill, a shelter was constructed at the west end of the mission church for him. After his death in AD 651, the wooden buttress he rested against was considered to have miraculous powers; it survived when the church was burnt down, not once but twice. This buttress is thought to survive today as a beam in the baptistery, over the font, where it serves no structural purpose.

The chancel is said to be built on the very place where St. Aidan died and just inside the chancel on the left hand side, this spot is marked. Behind it is a trefoil, a small window near the floor, which may possibly be a leper window to allow the patients from the leper hospital to observe the church services without entering the building.

In 1121, Henry I gave Bamburgh to the Augustinian Canons at Nostell in Yorkshire, the 'Black Canons', who benefited from this generous gift as the church and lands produced an income for the canons of about £600 a year, probably equivalent to over half a million today! Monasteries were lucrative businesses at this time, as they owned over one third of all the agricultural land in England. During the next hundred years or so, the church was gradually rebuilt to look much as it does today with the large, splendid chancel being built last, around 1230, mainly for the use of the monks.

The Parish Church of St. Aidan

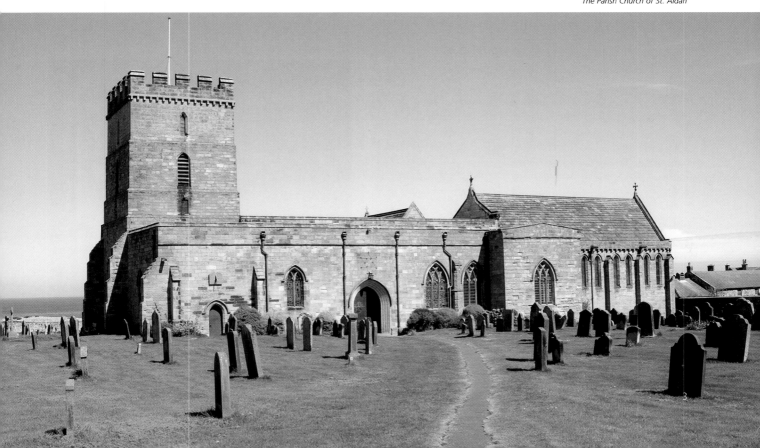

In the thirteenth century, the 'Black Friars', a Dominican preaching order, established a friary on what is now Friars' Farm. This had links to a convent dedicated to St. Sixtus and a leper hospital. By 1506, the Master of the Augustinians was so powerful that he considered himself also Master of the town and held manorial court on the site of what is now Bamburgh Hall. When Henry VIII dissolved the monasteries, the monks who had been in Bamburgh for 300 years were dispersed. Henry then sold all the Bamburgh lands and church to Sir John Forster who did little to maintain the church building.

In 1837, when rotten boards in the sanctuary were removed, a flight of stone steps was discovered leading down to a crypt where five coffins of the Forster family were found including the coffin of Dorothy Forster. The funeral helmet of Ferdinando Forster along with his breastplate and gauntlets are displayed on the north wall in the sanctuary.

In 1866, the rood screen was taken down and replaced with the present magnificent reredos, designed by H.L. Hicks of Newcastle and carved in stone from Caen in Normandy. The beautifully carved figures depict Northumbrian saints, including Saints Paulinus, Aidan, Oswald, Hilda, Cuthbert, and Bede. On leaving the chancel, do look at the fine fourteenth century hagioscope, a squint with a motif of thorns, allowing worshippers in the south aisle to see the high altar.

Opposite the entrance door, across in the north aisle is an effigy in memory of Grace Darling, which was originally in the churchyard but after the storm of 1885 when the canopy was blown down, it was brought inside for safekeeping and a new one placed in the churchyard.

There are many beautiful stained glass windows in this church including the third window after the effigy of Grace Darling. This is dedicated to the memory of Prideaux J. Selby, naturalist, who died in 1867; his grave is in the churchyard. By the age of thirteen, he had compiled notes on and illustrated many common birds. In later life, his books on Land Birds, Water Birds, and British Forest Trees were published.

Turning left from here you can see another fascinating window at the left hand side of the small altar. Messrs. Smith and Pawle of London designed it in commemoration of Annie Rochester, loving wife of Robert Stanley

Dalgliesh, who died on 2nd September 1937. Made 'In Honour of Women' it depicts six scenes of women saints and social reformers; 'a virtuous woman whose price is far above rubies', Proverbs Ch.31.

In the south aisle, next to the door, is Arthur Lionel Smith's memorial to his grandchildren who enjoyed family holidays at Bamburgh and died young. Do not leave without admiring the font with its beautifully decorated cover with its eight painted panels depicting the seven sacraments and profession of vows. Although at a glance it looks much older, it was given to the church by Caroline Thorp in 1852.

If you are now intrigued to know more about St. Aidan's Church and the Forsters there are two interesting booklets for sale in the church by John Bird: 'Saint Aidan's Church Bamburgh and its story through 1400 years' and 'Dorothy and the Forsters of Bamburgh'. The Forster family tree is displayed on a pillar near the font and you can buy a copy of this from the church. The welcome table by the door of the church is itself a piece of history as it was used in the church during Cromwell's time, when altars were forbidden.

When you leave the church there is usually a welcome bowl of water for dogs just outside. Now turn right and above the next door is a lovely sundial dated 1828.

The chancel with reredos

Grace Darling memorial window

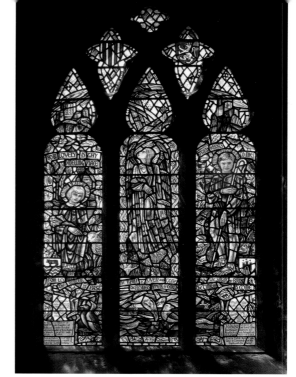

Window in memory of A.L.Smith's grandchildren

The Forsters

In 1547, Sir John Forster bought all the church lands in Bamburgh from Henry VIII but as he had no use for the monastery or Pele tower, he let them fall into ruin. In the seventeenth century, the stone was used to build the present Bamburgh Hall and farm buildings. The base of the old Pele tower can still be seen as part of the wall between the Hall and the churchyard.

Sir John has been described as arrogant, unscrupulous and out to make his fortune. During the Border Wars, he sacked and burnt sixteen border towns in 1559, as well as stripping the castles of Warkworth and Alnwick of everything of value. Therefore, it is not surprising that Bamburgh Castle was similarly treated and reported to be in a state of "utter ruine and decay". He was still involved in border clashes until the age of 70 and he died at Spindlestone in 1602. His funeral was a lavish affair and cost over £450, hundreds of thousands of pounds in today's money!

Sir Claudius Forster, already a wealthy landowner, was given Bamburgh Castle and its associated lands by James I. He died in 1623 and his memorial is one of the oldest in St. Aidan's church. His brother John inherited the estates but only outlived him by two years, and eventually William became heir while he was still a minor, but the estates were depleting in wealth due to the lack of personal attention and reduction in revenue as a result of the Civil War.

Sir William married Dorothy Selby and lived elegantly and extravagantly in

Bamburgh Manor (now Hall), which he rebuilt more or less in its present form. Bamburgh Castle at this time was largely in ruins. His daughter, Dorothy, received a proposal of marriage from Nathaniel, Lord Crewe of Stene, Lord Bishop of Durham, when she was eighteen, but she turned him down as despite his wealth she considered him too old at fifty-six. Lord Crewe married Penelope Tynte, a widow, but she died after a few years so he again asked Dorothy to marry him and this time, at twenty-eight years old and still unmarried, she said yes. They married in 1699 and when the Forster estates became bankrupt, Lord Crewe bought them from the receiver for £20,697, so in a way they stayed in the family. When all the debts were paid there was only £1,028 left for the Forster family.

Tom Forster and his younger sister Dorothy lived with their aunt, Lady Crewe, as their mother had died. Tom who became the General of the English Army during the 1715 rebellion was taken prisoner and ended up in Newgate Gaol in London. When his sister Dorothy heard the news, she was determined to help her brother. There are many different versions of the story but it is said that Dorothy set off from Bamburgh with the blacksmith from Adderstone in the depth of winter when the roads were covered with ice and snow.

A few weeks later, they arrived in London, Dorothy got hold of a duplicate key to his prison cell, and by bribery and guile got Tom shipped away to France. A mock funeral was held in Bamburgh with a coffin filled with sawdust, but Tom lived in France until he died in 1738. His body was then brought back to Bamburgh and buried in the family tomb in the crypt of the church. Dorothy married John Armstrong and when she died in 1767, she was also buried in the crypt. In the early nineteenth century, a coffin filed with sawdust that had never contained a body was found in the chancel of St. Aidan's church.

Above: Lord Crewe coat of arms

St. Aidan's Churchyard

The churchyard is dominated by Grace Darling's memorial, showing Grace with a carved oar by her side. This is a more recent carving, the original effigy being inside the church. Standing outside the church door and looking across towards the RNLI museum, you can see the tall cottage where Grace was born. It is the one with the slate roof three up from the RNLI museum.

Grace is a buried with her family in the small low-railed plot to the south. Suffering from tuberculosis, she came back to the village, where she died in 1842. The house, beside the telephone kiosk in the main street, where she died has a commemorative plaque above the door.

To the east of the Darling family plot, you will see, against the wall, a tall pillar, which appears to have been shattered at the top, an example of Victorian symbolism, commemorating a life shortened by tragedy. John Morell Mackenzie died at 36 years of age when the steamship *Pegasus* was wrecked on the Farnes in 1843. He was a professor of church history in Glasgow and as the ship sank, he collected the passengers around him and prayed aloud.

If you look right when leaving the churchyard you can see Glebe House, the original parsonage. The field between the two was where the vicar kept his horses in the eighteenth and nineteenth centuries. Further, up the road, on the left hand side is The Friars, the last house in the village, and it is thought to be the site of the Dominican friary.

Top: St. Aidan's Churchyard
Right: Effigy of Grace Darling
Below: Grace Darling Memorial in St. Aidan's Churchyard

In the middle of the seventeenth century, ornamental surrounds were added to the door leading to the chancel, probably by the Forsters, who lived extravagantly next door in Bamburgh Hall and who regarded the chancel as their own private part of the church.

The inscription on the third bell in St. Aidan's church reads:
"Lord may this bell forever be
Tuneful voice o'er land and sea
To call the people unto Thee."

RNLI Grace Darling Museum

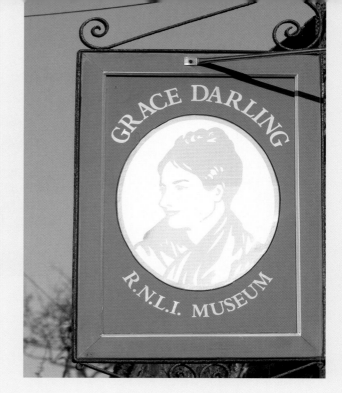

Opened in 1938 the museum is now managed by the RNLI Heritage Trust and is dedicated to the memory of Grace Darling (1815-1842). It has a unique collection of artefacts that commemorates Grace's heroism. At the time of writing in 2006, the museum was closed for major restoration work. All but the façade and the walls on either side of the forecourt were demolished and the new museum, which is due to open in the summer of 2007, will have two floors and offer new, improved exhibitions and displays as well as an educational and community room for research, events, talks and meetings.

Born on 24th November 1815 in her grandfather's cottage, just up from the museum, Grace, the seventh of nine children, spent the first years of her life with her family in a small cottage attached to the lighthouse on Brownsman Island out on the Farnes. Her father, William, was the lighthouse keeper here until 1826, when they moved to the newly built lighthouse on the island of Longstone.

On 5th September 1838, the steamship *Forfarshire* set off from Hull to Dundee. Her cargo included cloth, hardware, soap, boilerplate, and spinning gear along with about 60 passengers and crew. The next day the ship's boiler began to leak and by the 7th September, the engine stopped. Without any power, the *Forfarshire* began to drift. At about 4.00 a.m., she struck the Big Harcar rock on the Farnes and there was no time to call the passengers from their cabins and get them into the ship's lifeboats. Within fifteen minutes the ship had broken in two and the stern was swept away and sank with over 48 people on board.

Grace first saw the wreck at about 5.00 a.m. but at 7.00 a.m., when the stormy skies were lightening, amidst the huge waves battering Big Harcar rock she could see a few survivors. The storm was so fierce that William was sure it would prevent the launching of the North Sunderland lifeboat, so Grace and her father rowed out in rough seas to Big Harcar. Nine people were still alive on the rocks, but the coble could only take five in the first rescue attempt. While her father leapt onto the rocks to help the survivors, Grace had to keep the boat in place by herself by taking both oars and rowing backwards and forwards to prevent it from smashing into the rocks. They valiantly rowed back across the stormy sea to the lighthouse with five survivors, one woman, and four men. While Grace and her mother

looked after three of the survivors, her father and two of the rescued seamen rowed back once more through the perilous sea to save the other four men.

Grace became the first national and international celebrity created by the newspapers. Many artists came to the lighthouse to paint Grace's portrait, as everyone wanted to know what she looked like. She received hundreds of letters and presents, but did not enjoy all the attention.

Both Grace and her father were awarded honorary gold medals from the Royal Humane Society and silver medals from the National Institution for the Preservation of Life from Shipwreck (now the RNLI). Queen Victoria sent Grace £50.

Top: Grace Darling RNLI Museum / Bottom: Plaque on the cottage where Grace Darling died

Sadly, in April 1842, Grace became seriously ill with tuberculosis and she died on 20th October 1842. Hundreds of people flocked to Bamburgh for Grace's funeral and she is buried in St. Aidan's churchyard in her family plot. Two years later her memorial was erected in the churchyard, standing high so it can be seen by ships at sea.

Lucker Road

Heading west out of the village, bordered by the walled garden, is Lucker Road. There are shops, restaurants, hotels and guest houses. At the top of the road is the Mizen Hotel and there is some uncertainty about the origin of its name. One explanation is that Mizen is a corruption of 'Mizzen', meaning the head of a path, which leads down to the sea. On the other hand, it could be a corruption of 'Maison Dieu', which would connect it to the Dominican nunnery, dedicated to St. Sixtus and perhaps the leper hospital, which may have been situated near here.

Looking westwards from here you can see the low hill of Spindlestone Heugh where the mythical Laidley worm lived. The worm (or serpent) is the subject of an ancient ballad that tells the story of a beautiful princess who was turned into a worm by a wicked queen who lived in the castle. Only the princess's brother could save her and he set out from France to do so.

> *Banished to live at Spindlestone Heugh,*
> *Nigh a full league to the west,*
> *She coiled about the Spindle Stone*
> *And in a cave did rest.*

> *The milk of seven stately cows*
> *(It was costly her to keep)*
> *Was brought to her daily, which she drank*
> *Before she went to sleep.*

The queen tried to wreck his ship on the Farnes with a spell, but unfortunately for her the ship was made from rowan, which is protected from witchcraft, so he was able to rescue his sister.

> *He quitted his sword and bent his bow,*
> *He gave her kisses three.*
> *She shed the loathsome creature's skin*
> *And of the curse was free.*

The wicked queen turned into a toad and is said to live in the deep well of Bamburgh Castle.

> *Now on the ground near Ida's tower*
> *She crawls a loathsome toad.*
> *And venom spits on every maid*
> *She meets upon the road.*

Top: Plaque on the Grace Darling Museum / Above: Spindlestone Heugh

The Grove

In the centre of the village, on top of an old filled-in quarry is The Grove, a pleasant grassy space with a copse of trees, which is home to a large rookery and so can be quite noisy in the evenings!

The long narrow strip of grass now running the length of Front Street between The Grove and the cottages is where the medieval market was held. On the south side of The Grove are Grove Cottages; behind them is an old track used for access; originally all of these cottages had their own kitchen gardens which were assigned to them in medieval times. Beside the telephone kiosk is the small cottage, with a commemorative plaque above the door, which belonged to Grace Darling's sister and where Grace died.

At the top of The Grove, opposite the church, is the walled garden, which was originally used to supply the castle and Bamburgh Manor with fruit, vegetables and flowers and now you can by these and newspapers here. At the bottom of The Grove is the Lord Crewe Arms Hotel, a former coaching inn dating from the 1600s. In the reception area of the hotel there is a portrait of Dorothy Forster, Lord Crewe's wife.

The pant in The Grove / Below: The Victoria Hotel

The Castle pub, known locally as 'The Middle' still retains the stone steps leading up to the door, as well as its coaching entrance by the side that now leads to a garden, where children and dogs are welcome.

The Pantry is a delicatessen that sells a wide range of speciality groceries and Carters, a traditional family butcher, has been trading here since 1887. The village pump or the village pant, a Northumbrian dialect word for public fountain, can still be seen, with its drinking trough, at the end of The Grove.

The Wynding

Walking from The Grove towards the castle, on the left hand side, you come to a small road called The Wynding. In the nineteenth century, this was called Occupation Road.

On the left as you walk down The Wynding you will see the original village school, which had over one hundred pupils in the 1940s in three large rooms heated by stoves and open fires. This old school has now become a private house. Local children now go to school in Seahouses.

You will pass a row of traditional stone cottages and at the bottom of the road on your right; you will come to path leading up to the castle. Here you will find the old nineteenth century lifeboat station and this too has now become a private house.

Walk on round and the road dips and crosses the burn. Behind the wall on the other side is an international bird ringing station where important research on bird migration is carried out. Be careful if you continue walking up this road as it has a sharp bend, but you get superb views of the castle and the beach. Just below the squat lighthouse, you will see Stag Rocks, with a white stag painted on them, jutting out to the sea. There are series of rock pools here, and in the winter the end of the rocks becomes a favourite roosting place for purple sandpipers.

Above: Stag Rocks / Below left: The Old Lifeboat House in The Wynding

In August 1701, Ferdinando Forster was drinking at the Black Horse Tavern in Newgate Street, Newcastle, when his enemy John Fenwick of Rock came in, and the ensuing quarrel resulted in a duel. Ferdinando slipped and fell before he could draw his sword and, not waiting for him to recover, Fenwick ran him through with his sword and killed him. On the same spot a month later Fenwick was hanged.

Bamburgh Hall

To the east of the church is the private house of Bamburgh Hall, a seventeenth century manor house. The Augustinian Prior held his manorial court on this site in the Middle Ages and in the nineteenth century, what is now the dining room was used for the same purpose. Today it is Charles and Barbara Baker Cresswell's farmhouse and they offer bed and breakfast accommodation. The farm has a strong wild bird population and is a staging area for passing migrants, especially as Bamburgh is only two miles from the world-famous Lindisfarne National Nature Reserve and Budle Bay.

They have developed a cereal-based wild bird mix, using local ingredients, apart from a small amount of niger thistle seed included to encourage finches.

In the barn near the road, their shop, the Birdhouse, sells wild bird food, feeders, nest boxes, hand-painted china, books, and gifts. The artist Barbara Baker Cresswell is often in the shop painting china.

Bamburgh Hall

Armstrong Cottages

On the right hand side of the road on the way to Seahouses, you can see the green timbered buildings of Armstrong Cottages. These were built as inexpensive accommodation for the workers who were restoring the castle in the nineteenth century. Newer, modern versions have been built which blend in well with the originals.

Above and right: Armstrong Cottages

The Beach

The beach at Bamburgh is one of the finest in the country and is easily accessed from the car parking sites. The beach is renowned for its cleanliness and is one of six in Northumberland to be given 'Rural Seaside' awards. Swimming is generally safe, but do avoid places such as Budle Point to the north of the village when the tide is running. The water is cold and unless you are wearing a wetsuit you should treat it with respect. As the beach is long and flat, it is popular with sand yachtsman and horse riders, so do keep a look out when you are walking along. Please help to keep this beach clean by taking all your litter and glass bottles home with you.

This is a brilliant beach for dogs and was the first beach Ben, the author's (Catherine's) collie cross, ever set paw on. Please pick up after your dog on the beach and dunes and dispose of the bag in a doggy bin or take it home with you. I keep an old biscuit tin in the car for this purpose so that the car is not smelly!

Above and top: The dunes and beach between Bamburgh and Seahouses

Aerial view of Bamburgh (D Hunter)

The Sports Field

Situated beneath the castle is the village sports field used by the local cricket and football teams for matches and which is popular with residents and visitors. If you are walking your dog here, on the beaches or in the village, please pick up after you dog.

At one end of the field is Bamburgh Pavilion, built in the 1970s; it is used by sports teams and some twelve village groups, including the bird club, the Women's Institute, carpet bowls and yoga. Each September it also hosts the village show with prizes being keenly contested for classes such as cakes, homemade wines, fruit and vegetables and of course the Northumbrian passion, leeks. Beside the pavilion, there is a children's playground and hard tennis courts, which are available for hire by calling at the Victoria Hotel.

The raised path is a good place to look at the castle, where you can see, on the north end of the ramparts, a conical building, the remains of a windmill erected here in the eighteenth century by Dr. John Sharp, a Lord Crewe Trustee and Archdeacon of Northumberland. At this time when the castle and church belonged to the Trust, he also built a school for orphan girls inside the castle, as well as a public library, hospital, doctors' surgery and a hostel for shipwrecked sailors. There is a monument dedicated to John Sharpe in St. Aidan's Church.

Below the windmill is the watergate where Edward II entered the castle after the Battle of Bannockburn.

Above: The sports field below the castle / Below left to right: The war memorial from the sports field / The sports pavilion / The remains of the windmill at the castle

14

Bamburgh Castle

Bamburgh Castle dominates the coastline and the village, sitting on the summit of an outcrop of the Great Whin Sill over 40 metres above sea level. There has been a fortress where the castle now stands since AD 547 when a wooden palisade was built on the top of the crag. The castle's name comes from Bebba, the wife of Ethelfrith who ruled the kingdom of Northumbria from AD 593 until AD 616, and it soon became known as Bebbanburgh and then Bamburgh. From early times until the Normans rebuilt the castle in stone it was mostly a wooden structure.

After the Battle of Hastings in 1066 when William became king he recognised the importance of Northumbria as a buffer against the marauding Scots and granted it independence so there are no entries for Northumberland or Durham in the Domesday Book.

In 1095, the castle was held by Robert de Mowbray, Earl of Northumberland, as part of the rebellion against William II. The King besieged the castle and built a malvoisin nearby. When de Mowbray was captured, the King threatened to put out his eyes and so the castle, under the command of de Mowbray's wife, surrendered.

The keep, with walls over three metres thick, built in the reign of Henry II is shorter than those at Newcastle upon Tyne and Norham, as the height and strength of the rock made for safe entrance at ground level.

The castle featured prominently in the Wars of the Roses and was badly damaged by cannon fire in 1464 when the Earl of Warwick besieged the castle with 10,000 men and three huge guns. It was the first in England to be damaged and soon afterwards it began to fall into neglect. The building we see today is a combination of restoration by Lord Crewe, Bishop of Durham in the eighteenth century and by the First Lord Armstrong of Cragside, the Victorian industrial magnate, in 1894. His descendants have carried on the work and the castle remains the Armstrong family home.

The area around the castle makes for fascinating exploration; to the north the steep bank that marks the limit of the dunes is now thought by some archaeologists to be the original Saxon shoreline where boats were drawn up out of the water, whilst to the south ancient grave sites have been found. More information on this can be found in thecastle's archaeology museum.

Bamburgh is also perhaps the most iconic of Northumberland's historical sites and often is the first place to spring to mind when people talk of the county. This is no surprise, due to its popularity with film and television producers for making films such as *Ivanhoe* (1952), *Beckett* (1964), *Macbeth* (1972) and *Elizabeth* (1998).

The castle is entered from the south-east through the gatehouse, which looks Norman but was greatly restored in the nineteenth century, up a sunken road until you meet an inner gatehouse, called the Constable's Tower. Walk up into the open space that is the courtyard and the keep becomes visible. The remains of a twelfth century chapel lie towards the south end of the inner ward and recent ground radar searches and excavations have revealed a Saxon building lying under here.

It is well worth visiting the castle for, whatever your interest, it is most likely that you will find something here to grab your attention. On display are the impeccably neat exercise books from the charity school, Dorothy Forster's dress, a set of coastguard rules dated 1771, decorative china, French furniture, a tapestry from Aubusson and eighteenth century Venetian looking glasses and prints.

In the Kings Hall with its 'false hammer-beam' roof, there is a bay window with fantastic views of Lindisfarne and the Farne Islands, as well as a good display of armour. After gazing upwards at the elaborately vaulted stone ceiling of the porch, look around the walls and there are the portraits of Lord Crewe and his wife Dorothy Forster and her niece Dorothy, who helped her brother escape from prison. In the Faire Chamber is a painting of a country scene by Jan Brueghel (1601-1678). Russian prisoners of the Crimean War made the curtain in the passageway from their uniforms. In the keep, the scale of the fortifications of the medieval fortress can be appreciated, and here also are the massive chains used by Dr. Sharp to rescue ships.

The bakehouse and scullery have been restored to early twentieth century condition and are either historically interesting or they bring back memories!

Outside in the stable block is a Victorian paupers' hearse and do seek out the entrance door to the keep, with its unusual shape so that knights on horseback could enter withoutdismounting.

Above: Castle Gate
Right: Castle Keep from the village

If you are interested in science and technology visit the Armstrong Museum in the old laundry building, with displays and explanations of shipbuilding, armaments manufacture, heavy engineering and hydro-electric power. The exhibits in the Aviation Artefacts Museum all have connections with the Armstrongs or Northumberland and include salvage from wrecked aircraft from both World Wars.

When you have finished looking around make time for a visit to the tea room and the well-stocked gift shop. When visiting the castle it is best to use the castle car park.

BAMBURGH SERVICES:

Cash Point: In the bar of the Victoria Hotel.

Post Office: The village post office operates from the Victoria Hotel on a Monday and Thursday from 9.00 a.m. to 12.00 noon.

Post Box: The Post Box has a collection every day is in Front Street.

St. Aidan's Church: Please see notice board for times of services.

Toilets: Across from the telephone box on the other side of The Grove are the public toilets.

.

Shopping for Food:

R. Carter & Son, Family Butchers established 1887.

G.S. Clark & Son in the walled garden, greengrocer, plants and newspapers.

General Stores with an off-licence, gifts, souvenirs, and ice cream.

The Pantry is a delicatessen with nice cheeses, fresh coffee and a selection of groceries. There is a telephone box outside and a drinking bowl for dogs.

Gifts and Souvenirs:

The Copper Kettle Gift Shop has a lovely selection of cards, gifts and souvenirs.

The Bird House: Bird food and bird-related gifts.

Hotels and Places to Eat and Drink:

The Castle Hotel welcomes children and dogs in the garden. Telephone: 01668 214 616.

The Copper Kettle tea room has a small patio area at the back where children in pushchairs and dogs are welcome. You need to turn down by The Pantry, take the first left and walk along the back lane to enter the patio if you have a pushchair or a dog, otherwise you can walk through the tea room.

The Lord Crewe Arms is a hotel, bar and restaurant The Wynding Inn. No dogs allowed. Telephone: 01668 214 243.

The Victoria Hotel has a stylish mix of tradition and modern facilities; the bedrooms have recently been refurbished and some rooms have four-poster beds. Wedding ceremonies can be held here with receptions in the Brasserie. Facilities available for conferences and private dining. You can eat in the stylish Brasserie or in the comfort of the bar. Dogs are welcome in the bar and in some of the bedrooms. Telephone: 01668 214 431.

Attractions and Sports:

Bamburgh Castle is open from March until 31st October daily from 11a.m. to 5p.m. but it is wise to confirm this before arriving, as the dates can change. Telephone: 01668 214 515.

Bamburgh Castle Golf Club has been described as having one of the north-east's finest courses. A challenging par 68, it has dramatic views of the castle, Holy Island, the Cheviot Hills and the Farne Islands. Telephone : 01668 214 378.

Tennis Courts: The tennis courts are booked at the Victoria Hotel. Telephone: 01668 412 431.

Walking from Bamburgh to Seahouses

Dunes at Bamburgh

Walking between the two villages can be easily done along the beaches, but do check the tide table before you start, as the Spring Tides and even normal tides with a strong wind behind them can come right up to the dunes in certain places.

Bus timetables are displayed at the bus stops in Bamburgh and Seahouses and at the Tourist Information Centre in Seahouses. You can also contact Arriva busses on 01665 602 182 or Travelsure on 01665 720 907. Tide timetables can be found in the Berwick Advertiser and Northumberland Gazette, where the Holy Island crossing times are listed in the window of the Harbour Master's office at Seahouses as well as at the Tourist Information Centre.

From St. Aidan's Church, turn left down Church Street towards the castle. Just after the toilets turn left into The Wynding. Carry on along here until you come to the car park and walk onto the beach, crossing the Mill Burn where eider ducks and gulls are often seen drinking the fresh water. Walk along with the sea on your left and soon you will pass beneath the castle.

Don't rush this walk, take time to stop and admire the stunning scenery, the backdrop of this iconic castle, and the panoramic views along this walk. Every time you walk along here the scenery changes with the weather and on clear sunny days it has a Mediterranean feel about it, on misty days all the sounds seem muted, on gusty days it can be a noisy place with the crashing of the waves and the wind in your ears. On a cold wintry day, walking along the beach when darkness is falling in the afternoon, it is enchanting to see the lights shining from the castle windows and shadows creeping over the water.

Continue along the beach and you will soon see a large outcrop of rocks on your left and these are known as the

Islestone. They mark the eastern edge of the Parish of Bamburgh and are the closest point to the Farne Islands, visible from here. Behind you are Redbarn Links and you are now directly level with Armstrong Cottages and the large car park on the main road where there are toilets.

Walking along the beach, the foot of the old coastguard lookout tower comes into view and you will have to clamber over the rocks here. These are Greenhill Rocks and the steep path leading up through the dunes comes out opposite the road that leads up to Greenhill Farm. The dunes here are the tallest section along the beach, reaching some 30 metres high.

The beach seems to take a turn southwards and you will come to Monk's House, a group of houses set back from the beach so called because the monks of Lindisfarne took their supplies by boat from here to their cell on the Farne Islands. In 1257, Henry III granted the monks permission to build a storehouse for provisions at his 'mill at Brocksmouth', but the monks may have had a chapel here too, as Cuthbert Watson of nearby Shoreston Hall was buried here in 1597.

By 1893, it was divided into three houses, Brockhouse, Monkhouse and St. Cuthbert's Inn, and the 1943 census records ten people living here. Today they are private houses. In the 1950s and '60s, Dr. Eric Ennion, an influential naturalist and bird artist, ran a bird observatory at Monk's House for 11 years. His classic bird paintings have inspired generations of modern wildlife artists and his work has become very collectable. The story of Monk's House bird observatory is told in his book 'The House on the Shore', published in 1959.

Further along the beach are St. Aidan's Dunes, now in the care of the National Trust. Follow the line of the dunes until you come to the path that takes you up from the beach to the road at the north end of Seahouses.

Walk along the cliff top here and it is likely that you are following the way of an old cart track, possibly used by the quarrying firms to take stone to the harbour and to transport seaweed from the beach to the fields to be used as fertiliser. Cart tracks are still visible in the rocks below. On the other side of the road, there is a small post box in front of a large house that was built in 1914 for Captain and Mrs Buddle-Atkinson and called The Dunes. It was bought in 1930 and became The Dunes Hotel, with

dormer windows installed in the roof. Later, with the addition of the ballroom wing, many social occasions such as hunt balls were hosted here. The west wing was originally the servants' wing of the private house. The Dunes Hotel closed in 1982. It has since been converted into apartments.

As you get nearer to Seahouses, there are some flat greens in front of several houses, the Beach Hotel and St Aidan's Hotel. These buildings were erected in the early twentieth century and joined Seahouses with the small hamlet, St. Aidan's by the Sea.

Just along from here is the award-winning Seafield Caravan Park where you can hire a holiday home or pitch your touring caravan, and you can bring along your dog. Their Seafield Ocean Club has a health and beauty suite, swimming pool, gym and coffee shop and if you are a frequent visitor or live in Seahouses, you can join for an annual fee. The Seafield Restaurant with its lovely views is beside Seafield House, the one with a plough in its front garden. This is the original farmhouse of Seafield Farm.

After this is Seafield Park, with its Crazy Golf course and refreshments. A plaque on the wall tells you it was opened by the Lord Mayor of London. Just next door is HM Coastguard's office. Behind here are the public toilets, the Tourist Information Centre, a car park and the village of Seahouses, where you can rest awhile with a refreshing cup of tea, fish and chips or an ice cream after your long walk.

Seahouses harbour

Seahouses

Compared to other villages in Northumberland, Seahouses is a very young settlement. In 1887, a local guidebook described it as North Sunderland Sea-houses and as late as 1952 it was still being referred to as the small harbour of Seahouses at North Sunderland.

It is difficult to trace the origin of the fishing community, but in 1626, it is known that Shoreston and North Sunderland had seven resident fishermen. It is thought that when the fishermen living in North Sunderland grew tired of the long walk to the sea every day, they decided to build some houses down by the harbour to make their lives easier. These properties became known as 'the sea-houses'. In the late 1700s, the settlement was referred to as 'the sea-houses at Sunderland'.

In summer, Seahouses' harbour bustles with families and bird watchers on their way to the Farne Islands and divers making the most of the clear offshore waters. The village and beaches are alive with holidaymakers enjoying a day at the seaside, sampling the local fish and chips or strolling around the many gift shops.

Seahouses' permanent population of about 1,900 can easily treble during the holiday season. Although the village may have all the attributes of a seaside holiday centre with its fish and chip shops and amusement arcades, there is also a wealth of history here.

At first Seahouses' prosperity came from lime and the massive limekilns can still be seen set in the wall facing the harbour. Grain was another export and the granaries, up the bank from the Harbour Commissioners' Office and facing the harbour, are now apartments.

Above: Seahouses harbour
Right: Gull at harbour
Below left: Seahouses war memorial and roundabout

As in other ports in Northumberland, the herring was king here for many years. The Tourist Information Centre provides some excellent trails with information boards telling the story of the herring industry. Seahouses folk claim the kipper originated here when one of the herring store sheds caught fire!

Car Parking, Toilets and Tourist Information

The main Pay and Display car park at Seahouses is off the war memorial roundabout in the centre of the village. When you enter the car park, the toilets are on your right hand side. If you are staying in the area for a few days, it is worth considering a car park permit, available from the Tourist Information Centre, on the left hand side as you enter the car park, before you get your pay and display ticket from the machine. This weekly car-parking permit is valid in Berwick, Alnwick, and Morpeth council areas.

There is also a Pay and Display car park on the harbour run by the Harbour Commissioners and the money goes towards maintaining the harbour.

The Tourist Information Centre sells maps, cards, locally produced gifts, and interesting books about the area, as well as leaflets on places to visit and events. The staff, who are friendly and helpful, have a wealth of local knowledge and can assist with bed and breakfast bookings locally or in other parts of the country as well as times of local buses, trains, and tides.

If you enjoy a game of golf during your holiday, they have information on local golf courses and a three or five days 'Golfers' ParSport' is available.

A very useful leaflet on 'Heritage Walks around Seahouses and North Sunderland' is on sale here and it is a good introduction to the village and its history. The maps and route descriptions of the three trails are easy to follow and guide you around the information panels that are dotted about the harbour and the villages of Seahouses and North Sunderland. The Tourist Information Centre is open daily from 10.00a.m. to 5.00p.m. Telephone: 01665 720 884.

Above: Seahouses harbour / Below: Lobster pots at Seahouses

North Sunderland and the Old North Sunderland Railway

On the wall outside the Tourist Information Centre in Seahouses is a panel with information on the Railway Age. When you stand here, you are on the site of the railway sidings of Seahouses Station. Across the car park to your left is a red brick wall, which stands on the site of the platform; the paler bricks made up part of the platform's base. In the closing years of the nineteenth century, North Sunderland was the second most important fishing village in the north-east. To get the fish to market the North Sunderland Railway Act was signed by Queen Victoria in 1892; goods were first transported on 1st August 1898 and passengers on 18th December of the same year. The four miles of track from Seahouses connected with the Edinburgh-to-London mainline at Chathill. The line was operated by a single locomotive, a saddle tank engine, named *Bamburgh*, with five carriages, bought second-hand from the Highland Railway at Inverness. In 1934, a small diesel-electric locomotive named *Lady Armstrong* replaced the *Bamburgh*. The line was closed on 27th October 1951.

If you walk to the right hand corner of the car park, you can go through the gate onto a gravel track, which is a cycle path. This path takes you along the route of the North Sunderland Railway and eventually you arrive at a gate, which leads onto Broad Road in North Sunderland. The old North Sunderland Station was situated just across the road from here.

North Sunderland is the original village and still very much retains a separate identity, although it now forms one large settlement with Seahouses. The village was first known as Sutherlannland, referring to the land south of Bamburgh Castle, with the North being added later to differentiate it from the larger settlement on the river Wear in County Durham.

Turning left you will see the Longstone House Hotel, whose garden is the original village green. Stop at the junction and looking right and you will see the former Presbyterian Church built in 1810. The congregation now share St. Paul's Anglican Church.

Turn left and walking down the main street, on the other side of the road, you will come to a house set back; this was the Manor House, the oldest house in the village, dating from the seventeenth century. For a time in the nineteenth century it was the Blue Bell Inn and the Bronze Age pots found here may point to evidence of an even earlier settlement.

Just before the church is a hostel for groups visiting the area. It used to be a girls' school, set up by the Lord Crewe Trustees. You can recognize it by its large central ground floor window with small Gothic arched panes at the top. Across the road, what used to be the boys school is now the Lodge public house.

Like other settlements in Northumberland, the village suffered from raids by the Scots. The village had its own defensive Pele tower, which occupied the land where St. Paul's Church now stands and was demolished in the early years of the nineteenth century. Although built in the Norman style this church was designed by Anthony Salvin, the architect for the Duke of Northumberland and was consecrated by the Bishop of Carlisle on 14th January 1834. Just inside the cemetery gate is the grave of George Alexander Darling, Grace Darling's brother, a ship's carpenter who died in 1903 aged 84.

Top: Welcome to North Sunderland / Above: Longstone House Hotel

Along on the right you will come to Railston House, the house of John Railston, one of the richest men who lived in the village; he operated granaries on Seahouses' harbour as well as on either side of his house. On 20th November 1849, a raging fire destroyed a stable, a large granary, two cottages, and a valuable mare. The total cost of the damage was estimated at £300. Further along on your left are the remains of the village pump and the large double-fronted house just past the pump is the old Police Station. You are now leaving North Sunderland and as you pass Seahouses First School, with its centenary in 2006; you start to enter the land of guest houses and bed-and-breakfast establishments.

After the Second Word War and before the trend for package holidays in the 1960s, it was not unusual for families from Newcastle upon Tyne to come and spend the summer at Seahouses. These families wanted to rent houses and brought with them, or had sent on, lots of 'home comforts'. To accommodate this demand some of the Seahouses residents spent their summers living in their 'garden sheds' or outhouses and rented out their homes.

Eventually you will arrive at the Harbour Inn and continuing on down Main Street you will end up back at the Tourist Information Centre.

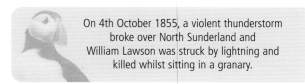

On 4th October 1855, a violent thunderstorm broke over North Sunderland and William Lawson was struck by lightning and killed whilst sitting in a granary.

Top: The Old Manor House, North Sunderland / Below: St. Paul's Church, North Sunderland

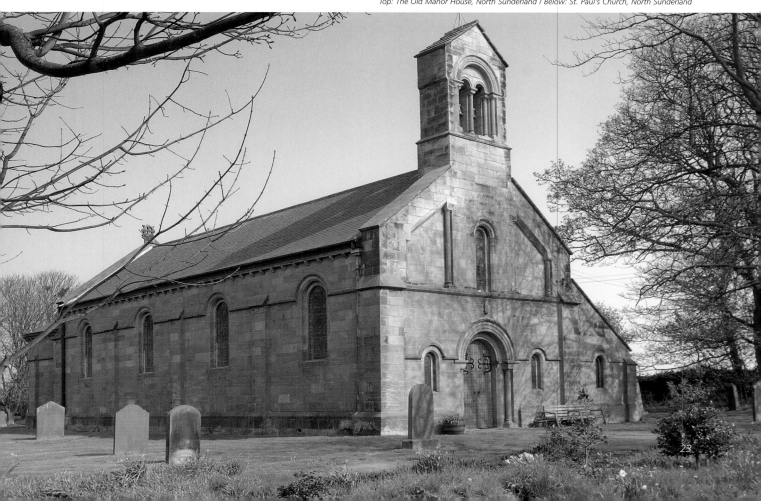

The Harbour

The most prominent feature in Seahouses is the harbour, although its correct name is North Sunderland harbour. The first pier of the modern harbour, financed by the Crewe trustees, was built in 1786 for the expanding lime trade, although there has been a port here since at least 1318. The export of coal forced the decision to build the major structures of the harbour, the North and East piers that we can see today. These were built at a cost of £25,000 and opened on 25th June 1889, when it was claimed that the harbour could take 300 fishing vessels.

While this work was in progress, it was necessary to store gunpowder for blasting the rocks. There was an anxiety that the gunpowder might explode and cause damage to the village, so a special store was built out on the rocks and it is still known as The Powder House. It stands in splendid isolation out on the rocks, to the far right as you face the harbour and is now a listed building.

The east pier was extended in 1933, and a hammerhead has been added across the north pier, which incorporates a flight of steps used at low tides by the boats carrying visitors to the Farne Islands.

On the south wall of the harbour, by the steps leading down from the village to the right of the Bamburgh Castle Hotel, is a small two-storeyed building that is the new North Sunderland Harbour Commissioners' Office, which opened in 2003. The weighbridge for the harbour used to be on this spot. The Harbour Commissioners manage the harbour and if you go on one of the boat trips, you will see that a few pennies from each passenger go towards the upkeep on the harbour.

Turn right at the Harbour Master's office and there is a row of cottages overlooking the slipway used for launching the lifeboat. Although they are much altered from their original appearance, these were the original 'sea houses' built by the North Sunderland fishermen and the village of Seahouses originated from this spot.

Sweeping away up the bank are apartment blocks with balconies that were originally built as granaries in the early 1800s. The grain trade was just as important as the lime

Left: The Powder House / Below: This building, now apartments, used to be the Wyvis Hotel

trade at this time and during 1846-7, thirty-one vessels carried more than one thousand tons of grain from here. One of the most important grain merchants was John Railston, who had a splendid home in North Sunderland.

On the cliff top, overlooking the harbour, is a large creamy-white house. This was originally the site of a herring yard, before Parsons, the Newcastle engineering firm built a house here. In the 1950s, it became the Wyvis Hotel, providing free holiday accommodation for employees of Leach Homes, a Newcastle building firm. Later, when Newcastle Corporation owned it, the elderly from Newcastle who would benefit from a holiday by the sea came here. It is now apartments with splendid views, and there is a good view of the Powder House from here. If you continue along a few metres, you come to a public coastal footpath and a caravan park. A little way along the footpath there is a well-sited bench with marvellous views across the harbour towards the Farnes and Holy Island.

This is a good vantage point to imagine the harbour filled with herring boats and the hustle and bustle of the catch being unloaded. The herring season started when the first shoals were seen off the Isles of Orkney and Shetland in the spring. They moved steadily down the east coast, reaching Northumberland in July and August, when there could be 300 hundred boats in the harbour. The herring were unloaded and taken to the ten herring yards, where gangs of women would split, gut, clean, and pack them into barrels of brine. This also kept the coopers of Seahouses busy making the barrels. Around 1834, over six thousand barrels of salt herring were exported to the Baltic States and Germany. The women followed the herring down the coast, often travelling from the Orkneys as far south as Great Yarmouth, and sometimes the local girls would join the gang, going with them when they left Seahouses.

As well as the large sailing ships that took herring, grain, coal and quicklime from the port, there was another type of boat that sailed the harbour. These were large model replicas of the herring boats, perfect in every respect from the red sails to the lead-lined keels. Most families had one of these model herring boats, which they raced across the harbour. As far as it is known, the only surviving example is held in the collection of memorabilia at the Olde Ship

The Olde Ship Inn

Seahouses harbour with the Farne Islands

Inn. This is not the only fascinating item displayed in this inn, as wherever you look there are models of vessels, displays of different types of knots, cases full of intriguing items, old photographs and a list of the Harbour Masters. Originally an eighteenth century farmhouse, the inn was first licensed in 1812; on the gable end the outline of the original building can be seen in the stonework.

You will often see eider ducks in the harbour, or Cuddy ducks as they are called locally, after St. Cuthbert who befriended them while he was living on the Farne Islands. Over the harbour wall, on the rocks below, you can sometimes spot redshanks, rock pipits, oystercatchers, grey herons and ringed plovers, sometimes known as the 'vicar bird' because of its white collar.

The Limekilns

Today the old limekilns by the harbour are mostly used for storage and garage space, but the top of the limekilns is now the garden of the Bamburgh House Hotel. The hotel building goes back as far as the early 1800s, and by 1899 it was an hotel. In its time, it has been a farm, the village school and a library, and the extension is built on the site of what was the village fire station from 1944 until 1960.

In Northumberland, where limestone was found in abundance, a local industry grew, with kilns supplying the surrounding areas with lime for the fields. The limekilns on Seahouses' harbour were some of the largest in Northumberland. As the agricultural revolution and new farming methods swept the country the demand for lime to improve the soil and increase the crop yield rose tremendously in the eighteenth and nineteenth centuries.

In places where the lime was near the coast, kilns were built at ports, such as Seahouses, Beadnell and Holy Island, as the lime could be loaded onto ships and carried to many destinations. In 1768, a lease was granted to quarry for lime south of the village at North Sunderland Snook, to mine the local coal seams for fuel and to erect the seven massive limekilns we see today. Lime was shipped to ports such as Perth and Dundee in Scotland, and other parts of the country, and in the 1850s the journey to Dundee took from nine to twenty-one days.

The limestone was brought to Seahouses by a rope-pulled wagonway, probably on wooden rails, from the quarries to the top of the kilns we can see today. The wagons were drawn up to the engine house, but used gravity to run down to the kilns. Part of the course of this railway can still be seen running across the golf course. Once at the kilns the limestone was placed in the chamber with the coal, where a temperature of 1,000°C could be reached.

Once the burning was complete, the lime fell to the bottom of the kiln, where it was raked out and cooled before being loaded onto the waiting sailing ships alongside the dock. In the ninety years the kilns were in operation the population of the harbour area grew to roughly five hundred. This in turn caused more housing and amenities to be built in the area. The kilns continued in operation until 1861.

The Limekilns at Seahouses Harbour

It is thought that the origin of the word kipper, used to describe smoke-cured herring, comes from the name given to the male salmon after spawning, as they are then pretty tasteless unless smoked or kippered.

The women and girls were paid by the number of herring they handled in a day and could earn as much as ten shillings a day (50p).

While waiting for the fish to arrive, the lassies would spend their time knitting traditional fisher 'ganseys'.

Walter White who visited Seahouses in 1858 wrote:

Lime is the principal article of trade; and the kilns are built close to the harbour for convenience of loading, and for the inconvenience of the town, which gets smothered with the smoke whenever the wind blows from the sea.

RNLI Lifeboat Station

The lifeboat station is open to the public daily and there has been a lifeboat here since 1827. The trustees of the Lord Crewe Estate operated three boats until the RNLI took over the station in 1852. The first boat used was some 30 feet long, self-righting, and powered by ten men with oars. That boat cost £150; compare that with the present boat, *Grace Darling* which cost £445,000 and would now cost over £1.2 million to replace.

The present boathouse was built in 1991 to house the *Grace Darling*, a Mersey class all weather lifeboat with protected propellers. She is relatively lightweight, which makes her suitable for carriage launching, although she is capable of operating from slipways and can lie afloat at berths. A small manually launched inflatable X boat is carried on board and is used to assist in rescuing casualties, as it can be rowed into areas inaccessible to the *Grace Darling*.

Grace Darling - Mersey class lifeboat
Length: 12 meters
Speed: 16 knots
Range: 140 nautical miles
Crew: 6
Launch method: Carriage, slipway or moored afloat
Cost to replace: £1.2 - £2 million

The lifeboat is transported on a carriage pulled by a tractor onto the slipway in the old harbour, where it is launched, so please make sure you take note of the signs and do not obstruct the road to the launchway. There is also an inflatable inshore lifeboat, which is transported on a carriage pulled by a Landrover onto the slipway for launching. A trailer is used for travelling by road when it is quicker to reach an incident than by sea, for example if the inflatable needs to be deployed on the Holy Island causeway. The lifeboats used to be called out mainly to assist trawlers and commercial vessels, but now the calls are mostly from pleasure boats, yachts, inflatables, and holidaymakers who disregard the Holy Island crossing times and become trapped on the causeway.

During Grace Darling's rescue, the North Sunderland lifeboatmen went out to the wreck in a coble rather than a lifeboat, as the coxswain, William Robson, thought it would be better suited amongst the rocks. With six men, one of whom was Grace's brother William, he rowed out to the wreck, but when they got there, all the survivors had been rescued. Unable to return to Seahouses because of the bad weather they made their way to Longstone, but

Top: RNLI sign at Seahouses / Above: The Grace Darling lifeboat at Seahouses (Liz Sanderson)

found the lighthouse was full so they were forced to spend two days sheltering in a derelict building.

The lifeboat station has an interesting gift shop and very helpful staff. It is open daily from Easter to October, during school half-terms and on the run-up to Christmas. You can contact the shop on 01665 721 604.

The Fishing Industry

In 1626, there were seven resident fishermen in North Sunderland, and fishing continues to play its part in the life of the village. The Heritage Museum is situated just opposite the Olde Ship Hotel and both are worth investigating if you are interested in discovering Seahouses' maritime past. The Heritage Museum offers an entertaining and educational experience about the fishing industry in Seahouses, with a full size fisherman's kitchen, smokehouse display, and tanks containing local fish, as well as other attractions.

Directly opposite the Heritage Centre is the Olde Ship Inn, which has an amazing plethora of brass and other marine artefacts in its main bar as well as scattered around the walls of other rooms. As the herring fishermen arrived from such ports as St. Ives and Inverness, the business prospered. Letting-rooms were made available as Seahouses popularity as a holiday destination increased. Indeed Sir William Russell Flint, widely acclaimed as the finest watercolour artist of his time, came to stay here in 1920. On the eastern side of the Olde Ship Inn, you will see oars and rudders from a coble, the traditional Northumbrian fishing boat.

Walk down the side of the Olde Ship Inn into Chapel Row and bear left. Here you pass some steep steps, called Malley Stairs, leading down to the harbour. Continue along Chapel Row and you will come to two stone pillars and a

narrow gap called The Nick. Look closely at the coping stones on either side of the gap and you will see the marks where the fishermen and their wives sharpened their limpet pickers, tools like bent chisels, used to extract the shellfish from their shells to bait the fishing lines.

Sitting side by side in front of you are the Black Swan Inn and the Schooner Inn. Richard Hall, shipping agent and grain merchant, built the Black Swan in 1843 and it is one of the earliest public houses in Seahouses.

You have now arrived at the old Seahouses, the centre of the herring fishing industry. The road facing you is North Street and on the left, you will see Union Street. A little way along Union Street on your left is Dawsons Square; the Dawsons were boat builders in Seahouses until the 1990s. Next, you come to Braidstone Square and these are two examples of the squares where fishermen and their families baited lines, repaired nets, prepared barrels, and generally put the world to rights in the shelter provided by the surrounding cottages.

Continuing along Union Street, you will come to South Street where you will find Swallow Fish Limited, where kippers and salmon are still smoked in the traditional manner in Seahouses' last fully operational nineteenth century smokehouse. Their shop, The Fisherman's Kitchen, has an interesting selection of the coopering tools that were used to make the herring barrels and a

display of photographs showing the history of fishing and kippering in Seahouses. You may be able to see the smokehouse and have the process explained to you by a member of staff. Groups need to make a booking by ringing 01665 721 052 or 720 580. There is a wide selection of locally caught shellfish and fresh fish as well as kippers and smoked salmon for sale. A mail order service is available so you can send some kippers to your relatives and friends all over the country. Have a look at the pair of coble oars above the door when you leave.

Further down the street, you will come to the picturesque Craster Square on your right, which originally was a granary. Turn left at 'Corner Cottage' and on your left, you will pass Sunnieside Square and lots of other interesting nooks and crannies in this small area. On reaching Crewe Street, admire the magnificent view of the harbour, the Farne Islands and Bamburgh Castle. Make your way back down to the harbour, turning left at the Harbour Master's Office and you will be back at the Olde Ship Inn.

Opposite: Seahouses harbour
Above left: Oars and rudders on The Olde Ship Inn
Left: Craster Square
Below: The harbour, with the harbour office to the right and much altered 'sea houses' to the left
(Photos: Liz Sanderson)

The Coble

The coble is the traditional Northumberland fishing boat, which evolved to suit the surf conditions of this coast and to launch and land on a level beach. However, as each generation developed sailing techniques the coble changed its appearance. A working boat carried four sails- a mainsail roughly rectangular and three jibs, one large, one medium and one small, known as the spitfire. Made of cotton the sails were tanned in boiling 'Burmese clutch' a tree extract from the Far East, which dyed them red. The cotton was dipped in seawater before dyeing in order to fix the colour and to stop it running.

A crew of four was the most efficient working number. Three men toiled away whilst the skipper would concentrate on sailing the vessel. All cobles carried two tillers, a short one for when working and a long one for sailing, as well as four oars made of spruce and approximately five metres long. About three metres of the oar was outside the boat and the last two metres were the long thin blades. When they were in use, the rower had to sit on the opposite side of the boat to compensate for the forces in play. You can see some examples of these oars on the side of the Olde Ship and above the door of Swallow Fish Limited.

The coble is clinker built with overlapping planks, with the bows moving in and out about a quarter of an inch. If not for this movement, the pressure from the waves would split the hull. Both masts were conical at the heel, which allowed them to turn in their sockets when the sail needed to be shifted from one side to the other.

Each mast also doubled as a bowsprit, the one being used depending on the weather at the time. Like the hull, blue and white seems to have been the favoured colour scheme for the mast and yards. Under sail, the coble was a very fast and lively boat; it took little to force her through the water, and at the turn of the century, wealthy Newcastle businessmen adapted them for racing.

In the hands of men who had sailed them all their lives, they came unscathed through the fiercest weather the North Sea could throw at them. It was inevitable that some would be lost, but this mostly occurred when coming to land. For a while, airtight wooden boxes were installed to aid buoyancy, but they took up a lot of room and at the end perhaps only about half of the boats carried them. You can see motorised working cobles further down the coast in Beadnell harbour and at Boulmer.

Sailing cobles often come back into Seahouses during the Seahouses Festival each year. Information about the festival can be found on the website: www.seahousesfestival.org or by contacting the Tourist Information Centre.

A fishing coble (Graeme Peacock)

The Farne Islands

The Farne Islands are owned by the National Trust and consist of a group of islands two and a half miles off Seahouses; of these islands between fifteen and twenty-eight are visible depending on the state of the tide. These are one of Britain's most important seabird sanctuaries with very friendly wildlife, allowing visitors close-up views. The name Farne is thought to come from the Anglo-Saxon word 'Farena' meaning 'pilgrim' or the Celtic word 'Fahren', a place of retreat.

There are two main groups of islands, the Inner Farnes and the Outer Farnes, separated by the Staple Sound and two outlying islands, Crumstone to the east and Megstone to the west. The closest is Inner Farne and the furthest out, at four-and-a-half miles from the shore, is Knivestone.

The Farnes are formed by the seaward outcrops of the Great Whin Sill, the volcanic intrusion that runs for over seventy miles across the north of England and forms the base for Hadrian's Wall. The rocks run from south-west to north-east and so they have rocky faces or cliffs on the south and west and slope gradually to the north and east. The Outer Farnes form the northernmost group and this is made up of Staple Island, Brownsman, Big Harcar, Little Harcar, Clove Car, North and South Wamses and Longstone.

The Inner Farnes make up the southernmost group and consist of East and West Wideopens, Little Scarcar, Big Scarcar and Inner Farne. Often referred to as Europe's Galapagos, the Farnes offer you an incredible experience, with over 100,000 pairs of nesting seabirds including 55,000 pairs of puffins. The best months to see the puffins are May, June and July.

The Farnes are reached by boat from Seahouses harbour, where you can book a visit from any of the boatmen's kiosks. If you are not a member of the National Trust, you will have to pay a landing fee when you visit Staple or Inner Farne islands. There is usually a stand on the harbour where you can join the National Trust, and if you will be visiting both islands and other places during the year it may be worthwhile joining here. No dogs are allowed to land on these islands; however, some of the boatmen are happy for dogs to stay on the boat whilst you visit, but be sure to make arrangements before you set off. To ease the pressure on the birds the opening times are staggered, with one island being open in the morning and one in the afternoon.

There are trips to Longstone, one of the Outer Staple Islands, from where Grace Darling made her famous rescue, and guided tours of the inside of the lighthouse. It is quite a gruelling climb up the lighthouse tower, so sensible footwear must be worn and children must be physically capable of climbing and descending the stairs unaided, as it is too dangerous to carry babies and children on these stairs.

Right: Catherine's dog Ben booking his boat trip
Below: Boat trip kiosks in Seahouses harbour
(Photos: Liz Sanderson)

Above: Trip boat in Seahouses harbour / Right: The Farne Islands (D Hunter)

bobbing up and down in the sea near the boat. He was all for having a swim himself, which of course is strictly not allowed. If you take your dogs on boat trips, you will need to keep a good hold of them and make sure they are well behaved. There was an interesting commentary from the boatman who was very knowledgeable about all the nesting seabirds and the history of the Farnes. On the way back, we saw a minke whale - that is everyone except Ben, who was tired out by then and fell asleep under the bench on the boat! We had a very relaxing and enjoyable afternoon and certainly recommend this boat trip.

You can take a boat trip to Holy Island, tides permitting. On the way you will sail around the Farne Islands and see the grey seals and many nesting seabirds before disembarking on the Holy Island of Lindisfarne where you will have about two hours to explore some of the many interesting places on the island, such as Lindisfarne Castle and the Priory. It may be worthwhile buying our guidebook 'Holy Island of Lindisfarne' by Steve Newman and Catherine Bowen (available from the National Trust shop in Seahouses and other good book and tourist shops) before you set out, and planning what to do during your visit as there is so much to see. On the way back, you will sail along the beautiful coastline, and the landward views of Bamburgh Castle and Lindisfarne Castle are magnificent.

There are cruises round the islands that take about one-and-a-half hours, and Catherine and her dog Ben went on Hanvey's 'Sailaround' on the *St. Cuthbert* as there was a sign saying dogs were welcome. There were two other dogs on the boat and we set out on a lovely sunny afternoon to cruise around the islands. We got amazingly close to the islands and some of the basking seals. There are nearly four thousand Atlantic or grey seals in the Farnes, and Ben found it quite exciting seeing lots of seals

If you are an enthusiastic ornithologist or photographer there are all-day excursions, about six hours in all, that go to both Inner Farne and Staple Island but there are no facilities except toilets on Inner Farne, so take water to drink and a packed lunch.

On the harbour, there are several kiosks where you can choose the trip and time that suits you. Billy Shiel's Boat

Trips have been operating from here for nearly ninety years. This enterprising family started taking boat trips of bird watchers to the Farne Islands after an early morning of hauling pots for lobsters and crabs in 1918, and a comprehensive package of trips is available today from this family firm on their boats, the *Glad Tidings*.

Hanvey's have been operating excursions to the islands since 1974 and offer a good range of trips on the *St. Cuthbert*. Golden Gate boat trips are the ones that offer the tour inside the Longstone lighthouse as well as other

excursions. Sovereign Boat Tours' vessel, the *Sovereign*, is fitted with a three-quarter shelter and an open rear, making it ideal in all weather conditions.

If you are a keen fisherman or diver, you can book a half-day or full-day trips to the fishing grounds or reefs and wrecks around the Farne islands or offshore from Alan Dawson or William Shiel.

The management of the Farnes

By 1840, the continued exploitation of the resources on the Farne Islands seriously threatened the seabird colonies, but fortunately Archdeacon Thorp employed wardens during the breeding season to safeguard the birds, and the Farne Islands Association, an organisation founded in 1881 by local people concerned about the seabirds, continued this important task.

In 1912, Lord Armstrong bought the Outer Farnes, and later, in 1925, the National Trust, following a public appeal, purchased both the Inner and Outer Farnes.

The Farnes are now one of the most important nature reserves in Europe, and the Trust's management plan tries to ensure that seals, birds, and human visitors benefit from their stay without the habitat being endangered.

Cormorants, shags and fulmars

The cormorant is a large, robust bird and the adults who look dark at a distance, have oily greenish-brown feathers on their upper parts and a large bill with a dark hooked tip. Mostly they are found on the Wames and East Wideopens, where the rocks are running with limewash and there is a fair amount of decaying fish, resulting in a particular indescribable smell.

The shags are smaller than the cormorants but also look dark despite having oily-green plumage, bottle-green eyes, a yellow gape, and an upturned crest. There are shags here throughout the year but not always the same ones! Some of the local birds move south and more northern birds take their place. The shags' untidy nests are constantly adorned with seaweed and have been found to contain such things as a rabbit's skull and a baby's comforter! There are now 1,000 pairs of shags, half of them on Staple Island.

The fulmar is gull-like but rides up-draughts on stiffly held wings, with the white-headed adults having a dark smudge through their eye. The first pair of fulmars nested on Inner Farne in 1935. They mate for life and greet each other with head-bowing and loud cackling. Only a single egg is laid on bare ground and if lost, they do not replace it. There are now about 250 pairs scattered over nine islands.

Inner Farne

Inner Farne has a landing stage, designated walkways, and a toilet, but due to the lack of electricity and fresh water there are no catering facilities here or on Staple Island. There is some wheelchair access on Inner Farne, but you need to contact the property manager well in advance of your visit by ringing 01665 720 651.

From May until July, the Artic Terns will be nesting near the paths, with eggs and chicks within inches of the board-walk. To protect their youngsters the adults will dive and peck your head; when this happens it is all too easy to step on chicks or eggs, so please wear a hat and watch every step you take, as the chicks move very quickly and often run towards your feet. Running or walking backwards, can be dangerous for you as well as the chicks. Please stand still while you are using a camera or camcorder to avoid any danger to the chicks. Remember the blue rope is there to protect the birds, so please do not cross this or put down bags or tripod legs beyond the rope. The island has some superb viewing points and you should be able to get close to puffins, sandwich, common and arctic terns, eiders, shags, guillemots, kittiwakes and other seabirds. There are few places where you can get this close to so many nesting birds.

Hermits and monks lived on Inner Farne for nearly 900 years and St. Cuthbert dwelt here from AD 678 to 684, returning just four months before he died on 20th March 687. His body was taken to Holy Island, but the monks were worried about Viking raids and so in AD 875 his body began an astonishing journey which lasted until 1070, when he was buried in what is now Durham Cathedral.

Inner Farne (Simon Fraser)

In the mid thirteenth century a small Benedictine community, the House of Farne, consisting of two monks and one or two servants was established. This House was endowed with goods and money from several benefactors, including Henry III, who donated the ground on the mainland, now Monk's House, on which to build a storehouse for supplies, and Alexander II of Scotland granted them eight shillings a year. The monks grew crops, kept livestock and poultry, sold seabirds' eggs, fish and seal oil, and made some money from collecting booty from salvaged wrecks.

All the buildings on Inner Farne date from the monastic period with the exception of the lighthouse. The small stone 'Fishehouse' by the landing is all that remains of St. Cuthbert's hospitium for his visitors.

By 1840, St. Cuthbert's chapel, completed in 1370, was roofless. Fortunately, the Archdeacon of Durham, Venerable Charles Thorp started a programme of restoration and purchased the inner group of islands in 1861. He salvaged some fine seventeenth century woodwork from Durham Cathedral and it now adorns this little church, although some of the angel heads were cut off and taken as souvenirs by minesweeper crews during World War I. The 1844 east window contains glass from William Wailes of Newcastle upon Tyne, whose work can also be seen in the Cathedral Church of St. Nicholas in Newcastle upon Tyne. The well-known Yorkshire craftsman, Robert 'Mousey' Thompson made the wooden altar furnishings, complete with his trademark, the tiny mouse; a further example of his work and his little carved mouse can be found in the choir stalls in the Parish Church of St. John the Baptist in Newcastle upon Tyne.

The defensive Pele tower was built in 1500 by Thomas Castell, Prior of Durham from 1494 to 1519 and it occupies the site of St. Cuthbert's cell. During the reign of Elizabeth I, it was used as a fort, and in December 1673, Charles II granted a licence for the first lighthouse to be established on the Inner Farne. It is thought that Sir John Clayton converted the tower into a lighthouse about that time, but due to a dispute with Newcastle merchants over dues for its upkeep it appears that the fire was never lit. Today it is the wardens' living quarters and is not open to the public.

William Shiel's boat Glad Tidings II leaving Seahouses on a trip to The Farne Islands (Liz Sanderson)

It was not until 1776 that Mr J. Blackett, in agreement with Trinity House, built two lighthouses, one on Inner Farne and the other on Staple Island. They were lit for the first time on 1st December 1778. Six years later the lighthouse on Staple Island was blown down in a storm and rebuilt, possibly on Brownsman, but this also succumbed to heavy seas in 1800 and was rebuilt once more on Brownsman. By 1809, both these coal-burning lighthouses on Inner Farne and Brownsman were in a state of decay and the running of them was taken over by Trinity House. The new Brownsman lighthouse was oil powered until it closed in 1826.

In 1811, the present lighthouse on Inner Farne, designed by Daniel Alexander, was built with its circular white tower, thirteen metres high. The lantern and gallery was installed with reflectors and Argand lamps. The keepers' cottages are to the rear of the tower and a stone wall surrounds the whole station. At the same time, a smaller lighthouse was built on the north-west point of the island and displayed a fixed white light. This light went out for the last time in 1910.

Alexander's lighthouse was converted to automatic operation, with acetylene light controlled by a sun valve until, in 1996, it was converted to solar powered operation and it is now controlled and monitored by a telemetry link from Trinity House Operations Control Centre at Harwich. It flashes two white and red lights every fifteen seconds. The white light can be seen for ten sea miles and the red for seven sea miles. This lighthouse is not open to the public.

Staple Island

Staple Island is accessed by steps and is a rocky place, so do take care when on the island. This trip is not recommended for visitors with walking difficulties. There are no toilets or catering facilities on this island, so take some water with you. As the island is very exposed to the elements, landing can occasionally be difficult, and it is always a good idea to ask about the weather and sea conditions before sailing. Landings are made at the discretion of the boat's skipper.

There is a superb viewing platform, where you can see the birds up close, and the cliff scenery around the three pinnacles, which are over twenty metres high, is well worth the boat trip. There was a fourth pinnacle but it was destroyed by a storm in the nineteenth century. This is an ideal trip for birdwatchers, with fantastic photographic opportunities. Staple Island's first purpose-built lighthouse was a square tower; it was blown down by gale force winds in 1784.

To the east of the island is the small island of Brownsman, with the remains of the old 1810 lighthouse and cottage. This is where Grace Darling lived with her father before moving out to Longstone. By 1824, it was thought that the position of the Brownsman light was not good enough to protect shipping, as the treacherous rocks extended one-and-a-half miles out to sea. The following year work started on the new Longstone lighthouse, and William Darling, the lighthouse keeper, and his family moved to Longstone in 1826.

Kittiwake and eggs (Simon Fraser)

Gulls

The kittiwakes are delightful birds, and there are over 6,000 pairs, with their nests precariously stuck to the rock faces. You can recognise them in summer by their bright white heads, necks, rumps and tails, pale ashy blue-grey backs and upper wings with neat black wing tips.

The lesser black-backed and herring gulls nest mainly on rocky islands, such as the Wamses, Harcars and Wideopens. These are predatory birds, and their numbers have been on the increase, although measures are now taken to keep them in check.

The black-headed gulls were once rare, but they are now nesting in increasing numbers near the tern colonies. In summer, the adults' heads are a dark chocolate brown with the colour extending to the middle of the head but not down the back of the neck.

Longstone Island

Longstone has a landing stage, with paths of concrete and tarmac; there is no landing fee here as it is not a bird sanctuary. Dogs can disembark here but cannot go on the lighthouse tour. Longstone lacks the cliffs of Staple and Inner Farne so the bird life is not so rich, as in rough weather the sea can swamp the island.

The lighthouse, a red and white circular tower, some twenty-six metres high, built of rough stone with iron railings around the lantern gallery, was designed and built by Joseph Nelson. In 1826, the light came from Argand lamps with twelve burners, parabolic reflectors some twenty-one inches in diameter and nine inches deep, and a catadioptric optical apparatus. The cost of the lighthouse and dwellings was £4,771.

The storms could be so dreadful that many a time the family had to seek refuge in the upper rooms of the tower as the living quarters were lashed by the pounding waves.

Major alterations were made to the lighthouse in 1950, when the light was converted to electricity. It was converted to automatic operation in September 1990 and is now monitored from the Trinity House Operations Control Centre at Harwich in Essex. The white light, which flashes every twenty seconds, can be seen for twenty-four sea miles and the fog signal sounds two blasts every sixty seconds.

Seals

The Atlantic grey seal (Halichoerus grypus) is the rarest species of seal in the world and the largest surviving carnivore in the British Isles, so this colony is one of the most important in Europe, as there are now 3,000 - 4,000 seals, with about 1,000 pups being born each year in late October and November. A mature bull can weigh up to three hundred kilograms.

Although on land they move about with looping caterpillar-like action, flopping along on their stomachs, they are graceful and adept underwater swimmers. Seals are inquisitive and seem to enjoy watching the boats and passengers as much as they enjoy watching them! As they remain vertical in one spot the seals' faces with their narrow nostrils and moustaches, pop up through the waves for a good look. Young seals are very curious and will approach and follow divers.

Seals used to be an important source of oil and skin, but the 1932 Grey Seals Protection Act limited these activities. It is said that in foggy weather their moans serve as a warning to vessels sailing too close to the islands.

Longstone lighthouse with Atlantic grey seals (Simon Fraser)

Eider ducks

St. Cuthbert was fond of the eider duck and according to Eddius, a monk, 'they were so tame that they would allow themselves to be stroked and petted, would come running when he called and would build their nests under his bed'. Locally these ducks are called Cuddy ducks after St. Cuthbert who laid down rules to protect them during the breeding season.

They are usually found against dry stone walls or amongst vegetation. Eiders are present around the islands throughout the year and the black and white drakes, with their lime green markings and pink flush on their breasts, do not stay around waiting for their brood to hatch. The female has mottled brown plumage, and a non-breeding duck acts as a sort of 'auntie' as immediately on hatching the ducklings are led to the sea.

Terns

The terns are very graceful birds that dive and wheel against the sky. During the winter, they migrate, mainly to the coasts of Africa, with the exception the Artic tern, which performs the longest migration of any bird as it flits between the North and South Poles, stopping off at the Farne Islands during the summer.

The Artic terns usually return to their birthplace to build their nests and are very protective of them. They are experts at dive-bombing attacks to defend their nests from visitors and there are up to 4,000 of them on Inner Farne and Brownsman.

The Sandwich terns are temperamental birds and there is no knowing where they will build next year's nest, but there are usually about 2,000-3,000 pairs nesting on the Farne Islands.

Auks

In the eighteenth century, there were great auks on the Farne Islands, but sadly they are now extinct.

Over 15,000 breeding pairs of guillemots are found in the Farne Islands, particularly on the pinnacles off Staple Island.

They lay one pointed-shaped egg that rolls in a narrow circle so preventing it rolling into the sea from the bare rock.

A few weeks after the chicks hatch and before they can fly, they jump off the rock into the water, where their parents teach them how to feed.

Razorbills, unlike guillemots, are solitary, preferring a ledge to themselves. There were over 150 breeding pairs in 2005, mostly on Inner Farne.

Little auks, black and Brunnich's guillemots appear occasionally.

Top: Guillemots at the Farnes / Below: Eider ducks at the Farne Islands (Simon Fraser)

Diving and Shipwrecks

William Shiel with his boat Glad Tidings and divers in Seahouses harbour
(Liz Sanderson)

The *Forfarshire* may well be the most famous of the wrecks on the Farnes but she is only one of hundreds of vessels that have sunk here. Although many of these wooden vessels have disappeared, a surprising number of metal-built ships from the nineteenth century onwards have created artificial reefs for the marine life and can be visited by experienced divers who have studied the wrecks and know the local tidal conditions.

The scattered remnants of some of these wrecks lie in the thick kelp forests that surround the islands, but others are in fairly open water. The *Emma*, a Swedish steamship, built in 1892, was driven onto the Knivestone rocks on 9th December 1914 en route to Manchester from Sweden with a cargo of wood pulp, oil, cast iron ingots and pigs, and a crew of twenty. Her remains are mixed up with those of the *Abessina*, locally known as the '*Abyssinia*', a German steamship, that was stranded on the Knivestone Reef in September 1921 and became a total wreck. There is plenty of marine life around these wrecks and young grey seal pups often follow the divers around.

The *Helmsdale*, on the other hand, has now been pounded by storms and totally fragmented, so much so that the wreckage is spread over a large area and is under a thick carpet of kelp. She was on her way from London to Inverkeithing with a cargo of cement when in thick fog she was grounded on the shallow reefs off Crumstone on 19th July 1939. Her crew were rescued, but she was badly damaged and quickly broke up.

The Guide Me in Seahouses Harbour (Liz Sanderson)

During the First and Second World Wars, German submarines operated along the coast, and this resulted in many more wrecks from both sides.

The *Athelduke*, an 8,966-ton motor tanker, was torpedoed by the German submarine U1274 on 16th April 1945 about five-and-a-half miles from Longstone. She was carrying a cargo of molasses, four gunners, four passengers and a crew of 43. The ship remained afloat for some time before she finally sank and on hitting the seabed broke in two. The two sections of this wreck are enormous, but at a depth of 55 metres, with dangerous currents, in direct line with the main shipping lane and a cobweb of trawler nets draped over the structure, it could be a seriously hazardous dive.

After sinking the *Athelduke*, the U1274, German Kriegsmarine U-boat was pursued by the British escorting destroyer HMS *Viceroy* which attacked and sank her with depth charges. To make sure the U-boat had been destroyed the *Viceroy* returned a few days later and dropped more depth charges until proof could be seen that it had broken up. The wreck of the U1274, seven-and-a-half miles off Longstone, is standing upright and is still intact except for her stern end, which was probably damaged by the depth charges. The hatches are still sealed but as this is a war grave, entering the boat would not only be morally wrong but also against the law.

One of the best dives is said to be the *Somali*, a passenger and cargo steamer built in 1939 and sunk in March 1941 after being bombed by a German Heinkel 111. The *Somali* sits upright in 30 metres of water, with much of the 450 ft hull still intact it makes an impressive slack-water dive. Dives can be arranged with Alan Dawson on his boat *Guide Me* or with William Shiel who has two boats operating out of Seahouses harbour with dive lifts fitted for easy access to the water. The National Trust shop in Seahouses has books, gifts and souvenirs of the Farne Islands.

SEAHOUSES SERVICES

Cash Points: Barclays Bank near the Tourist Information Centre and in the wall of the Co-op.

Chemist: Longstone Pharmacy, 32 Main Street. Please see shop for opening times. Tel: 01665 720 228

The Health Centre: James Street, Seahouses. Tel: 01665 720 294 or 720 917

Internet Access: North Sunderland and Seahouses Development Trust: Entrance at the rear of the building. Open weekdays from 9.30 a.m. to 4.30 p.m. for internet access, photocopying and laminating. Computer courses and classes on other topics are run here and you are welcome to call in for details, or ring 01665 721 868.

Library: For details of opening times ring 01665 720 923.

Police Station: 01665 720 204. Non-emergencies 101. Emergencies 999.

Post Office: Open Monday to Friday 9.00a.m.-12.30pm and 1.00-5.00p.m. Closes for lunch 12.30 - 1.00pm, closed Wednesday and Saturday afternoons. It is near the Harbour Inn on the road to Beadnell.

St. Aidan's Catholic Church: an interesting redbrick building. Times of services are displayed on the notice board.

Methodist Church is in the Main Street in Seahouses and details of services are on their notice board.

St. Cuthbert's United Reformed Church meets in St. Paul's Church in North Sunderland and details of services are on their notice board.

The Parish Church of St. Paul is in North Sunderland and details of their services are on their notice board.

Shopping for Food:

The Co-op - Seahouses' Supermarket.

The Fisherman's Kitchen - in South Street, for fresh fish, smoked salmon and kippers.

Geo. Scott & Son - family butchers since 1883.

The Northumbrian Hamper - Farm shop with local produce and well-presented gift hampers.

Trotters Family Bakers - for a good variety of bread, tempting cakes, and buns.

Gifts and Souvenirs:

Farne Gift Shop - an Aladdin's cave of gifts, toys, souvenirs and all sorts of things.

Linen and Lace - Tablecloths, runners, bedspreads, and many pretty gifts.

The National Trust Shop - with a range of quality gifts, local books, cards and especially items linked to the Farne Islands.

Polka Dots: Gifts, souvenirs, cards, prints & paintings.

RNLI Shop in Seahouses Lifeboat Station for seafaring gifts.

Shoreline Gifts - Gifts, souvenirs and cards with a nautical theme.

Newsagents and Books:

Corklee News: As well as newspapers and magazines there is also an off-licence and videos to rent.

T.T. Cuthbertson Newsagent with cards, maps, and sweets.

Barter Books: Second-hand bookshop. Opening times are displayed in the shop.

Other Shopping:

Amber's Holistic Beauty Salon is just the place for a relaxing treat during your holiday. Telephone number: 01665 721 995

Newton's Electrical Appliances - also does repairs and has a video library.

Fancy Goods and Hardware - opposite the Harbour Inn has an interesting mix of hardware and kitchen items.

Pennywise - is like a mini department store with clothing for the whole family, haberdashery, shoes, party things and a dry cleaning and shoe repair service.

Raggy Dolls - for sunhats and women's clothing.

Pet Care:

Aln Veterinary Surgery: This surgery is not open every day, but the times are displayed. They are a well-established and reputable practice with the main surgery in Wagonway Road in Alnwick. Telephone number for Seahouses surgery: 01665 721 800. Alnwick surgery: 01665 510 999

Alnwick Dog Grooming: Recommended by Ben, Catherine's collie cross, as he had his coat trimmed, claws clipped, and a bath here during the hot weather in 2006 and loved his new, much cooler, look! The Pet Shop has a good variety of dog and cat food, collars and leads and pet toys.

Attractions, Sports & Trips:

Heritage Centre and Museum: The museum has models of ships, a fisherman's kitchen, displays showing how the barrels for the salt herring were made and information on the Farne Islands. The shop has children's toys, gifts, and souvenirs.

Seafield Park with a popular Crazy Golf course and refreshments.

Seahouses Golf Club is an eighteen hole course with a standard scratch of 67 and two of the most prestigious par threes in the north of England. It is just south of the village on either side of the B1340 Alnwick Road. From the course, there are splendid views of Dunstanburgh castle, Bamburgh castle and the Farne Islands. Visitors are welcome at the club. Telephone: 01665 720 794.

Sports Centre: facilities include floodlit tennis courts, indoor and outdoor bowls, and badminton. Tennis courts and bowling greens can be booked by the hour. Contact 01665 721 868.

Travelsure: Day excursions, British and European holidays.

Farne Island Boat Trips:

Boat trips to the Farne Islands, Holy Island, and fishing and diving grounds can be booked from Seahouses Harbour.

Alan Dawson: Diving and Angling Trips: ring 01665 720 940

Billy Shiels Boat Trips: ring 01665 720 308

Golden Gate Boat Trips and Tours of Longstone Lighthouse: ring 01665 721 210

Hanvey's Boat Trips: ring 01665 720 388

Sovereign Boat Tours: ring 01665 721 667

William Shiels Diving Trips: ring 01665 721 297

Hotels and places to eat and drink:

Bamburgh Castle Hotel and Restaurant has 20 rooms, including sea-facing four-poster rooms, and the restaurant, open to non-residents, has good views over the harbour. The site of the garden is quite unusual as it is on the top of the old limekilns. Ring 01665 720 283.

The Beach Hotel: on the seafront has fourteen rooms. Children welcome. Telephone 01665 720 337.

The Black Swan Inn: one of the oldest in Seahouses.

Coxon's Ice Cream & Coffee Bar has served delicious homemade ice creams in Seahouses for generations.

The Harbour Inn: on the roundabout between Seahouses and North Sunderland. Telephone 01665 720 600.

Koffee & Kreme has seating outside in the summer.

Lewis's Fish Restaurant to sit in or take away.

The Links Hotel in King Street. Telephone 01665 720 062.

The Lodge Pub, North Sunderland used to be a boy's school.

Longstone House Hotel, North Sunderland, bar and restaurant, children and dogs welcome. Telephone 01665 720 212.

Mackays Fish and Chips: established in 1926, next to the Farne Gift Shop.

Neptune Fish Restaurant

The Olde Ship Inn with real ale and bar meals served in atmospheric surroundings, as everywhere there are memorabilia of ships and seafarers, in display cases, on the walls and hanging from the ceiling. Rooms available - no dogs or children under 10 years. Telephone 01665 720 200.

Pinnacles Fish and Chips: restaurant and take-away.

Rosemary's Tea Room: also serves breakfast.

The Seafield Restaurant

The Schooner Inn

The Seafarers Café & Restaurant

St. Aidan's Hotel on St. Aidan's seafront has eight rooms and welcomes well-behaved pets by arrangement. Telephone 10665 720 355.

Caravan Park:

Seafield Caravan Park with holiday homes and a tourer site welcomes children and dogs. Their Ocean Club facilities include a twenty-metre swimming pool, spa area, fitness suite, and health and beauty suite. Telephone 01665 720 628.